Zodiac Charted designs

FOR CROSS-STITCH, NEEDLEPOINT AND OTHER TECHNIQUES

from the archives of the

Lindberg Press

DOVER PUBLICATIONS, INC.
New York

Copyright © 1985 by Dover Publications, Inc.
All rights reserved under Pan American and International Copyright Conventions.

Published in Canada by General Publishing Company, Ltd., 30 Lesmill Road, Don Mills, Toronto, Ontario.
Published in the United Kingdom by Constable and Company, Ltd., 10 Orange Street, London WC2H 7EG.

Zodiac Charted Designs for Cross-Stitch, Needlepoint and Other Techniques is a new work, first published by Dover Publications, Inc., in 1985.

Manufactured in the United States of America
Dover Publications, Inc., 31 East 2nd Street, Mineola, N.Y. 11501

Library of Congress Cataloging in Publication Data
Main entry under title:

Zodiac charted designs for cross-stitch, needlepoint, and other techniques.

(Dover needlework series)
"From the archives of the Lindberg Press."
1. Needlework—Patterns. 2. Zodiac. I. Lindberg Press. II. Series.
TT753.Z63 1985   746.4   85-6813
ISBN 0-486-24932-8

introduction

Here are five new sets of zodiac charts—that's sixty designs—from the needles and pens of top-flight modern Danish artists. The designs can be used as you please: a motif on a table napkin, a pretty picture to brighten a drab corner, a needlepoint pillow, a blouse pocket, a tennis-racket cover. Anywhere you can stitch, you can add your Taurus, Libra or Leo.

Most of these designs were originally created for counted cross-stitch, but they are easily translated into other needlework techniques. Keep in mind that the finished piece will not be the same size as the charted design unless you are working on fabric or canvas with the same number of threads per inch as the chart has squares per inch. With knitting and crocheting, the size will vary according to the number of stitches per inch.

COUNTED CROSS-STITCH

MATERIALS

1. **Needles.** A small blunt tapestry needle, No. 24 or No. 26.

2. **Fabric.** Evenweave linen, cotton, wool or synthetic fabrics all work well. The most popular fabrics are aida cloth, linen and hardanger cloth. Cotton aida is most commonly available in 18 threads-per-inch, 14 threads-per-inch and 11 threads-per-inch (14-count is the most popular size). Evenweave linen comes in a variety of threads-per-inch. To work cross-stitch on linen involves a slightly different technique (see page 5). Thirty thread-per-inch linen will result in a stitch about the same size as 14-count aida. Hardanger cloth has 22 threads to the inch and is available in cotton or linen. The amount of fabric needed depends on the size of the cross-stitch design. To determine yardage, divide the number of stitches in the design by the thread-count of the fabric. For example: If a design 112 squares wide by 140 squares deep is worked on a 14-count fabric, divide 112 by 14 (=8), and 140 by 14 (=10). The design will measure 8″ × 10″. The same design worked on 22-count fabric measures about 5″ × 6½″.

3. **Threads and Yarns.** Six-strand embroidery floss, crewel wool, Danish Flower Thread, pearl cotton or metallic threads all work well for cross-stitch. DMC Embroidery Floss has been used to color-code the patterns in this volume; a conversion chart for Royal Mouliné Six-Strand Embroidery Floss from Coats & Clark, and Anchor Embroidery Floss from Susan Bates appears on page 7. Crewel wool works well on evenweave wool fabric. Danish Flower Thread is a thicker thread with a matte finish, one strand equaling two of embroidery floss.

4. **Embroidery Hoop.** A wooden or plastic 4″, 5″ or 6″ round or oval hoop with a screw-type tension adjuster works best for cross-stitch.

5. **Scissors.** A pair of sharp embroidery scissors is essential to all embroidery.

PREPARING TO WORK

To prevent raveling, either whip stitch or machine-stitch the outer edges of the fabric.

Locate the exact center of the chart (many of the charts in this book have an arrow at the top and side; follow these arrows to their intersection to locate the chart center). Establish the center of the fabric by folding it in half first vertically, then horizontally. The center stitch of the chart falls where the creases of the fabric meet. Mark the fabric center with a basting thread.

It is best to begin cross-stitch at the top of the design. To establish the top, count the squares up from the center of the chart, and the corresponding number of holes up from the center of the fabric.

Place the fabric tautly in the embroidery hoop, for tension makes it easier to push the needle through the holes without piercing the fibers. While working continue to retighten the fabric as necessary.

When working with multiple strands (such as embroidery floss) always separate (strand) the thread before beginning to stitch. This one small step allows for better coverage of the fabric. When you need more than one thread in the needle, use separate strands and do not double the thread. (For example: If you need four strands, use four separated strands.) Thread has a nap (just as fabrics do) and can be felt to be smoother in one direction than the other. Always work with the nap (the smooth side) pointing down.

For 14-count aida and 30-count linen, work with two strands of six-strand floss. For more texture, use more thread; for a flatter look, use less thread.

EMBROIDERY

To begin, fasten the thread with a waste knot and hold a short length of thread on the underside of the work, anchoring it with the first few stitches (*Diagram 1*). When the thread end is securely in place, clip the knot.

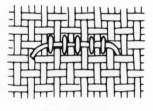

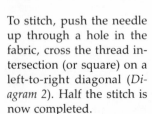

DIAGRAM 1
Reverse side of work

To stitch, push the needle up through a hole in the fabric, cross the thread intersection (or square) on a left-to-right diagonal (*Diagram 2*). Half the stitch is now completed.

Next, cross back, right to left, forming an X (*Diagram 3*).

DIAGRAM 2

DIAGRAM 3

DIAGRAM 4

Work all the same color stitches on one row, then cross back, completing the X's (*Diagram 4*).

Some needleworkers prefer to cross each stitch as they come to it. This method also works, but be sure all of the top stitches are slanted in the same direction. Isolated stitches must be crossed as they are worked. Vertical stitches are crossed as shown in *Diagram 5*.

DIAGRAM 5

At the top, work horizontal rows of a single color, left to right. This method allows you to go from an unoccupied space to an occupied space (working from an empty hole to a filled one), making ruffling of the floss less likely. Holes are used more than once, and all stitches "hold hands" unless a space is indicated on the chart. Hold the work upright throughout (do not turn as with many needlepoint stitches).

When carrying the thread from one area to another, run the needle under a few stitches on the wrong side. Do not carry thread across an open expanse of fabric as it will be visible from the front when the project is completed.

To end a color, weave in and out of the underside of the stitches, making a scallop stitch or two for extra security (*Diagram 6*). When possible, end in the same direction in which you were working, jumping up a row if necessary (*Diagram 7*). This prevents holes caused by stitches being pulled in two directions. Trim the thread ends closely and do not leave any tails or knots as they will show through the fabric when the work is completed.

A number of other counted-thread stitches can be used in cross-stitch. Backstitch (*Diagram 8*) is used for outlines, face details and the like. It is worked from hole to hole, and may be stitched as a vertical, horizontal or diagonal line.

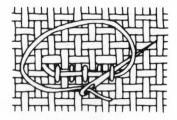

DIAGRAM 6
Reverse side of work

DIAGRAM 7
Reverse side of work

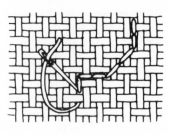

DIAGRAM 8

Straight stitch is worked from side to side over several threads (*Diagram 9*) and affords solid coverage.

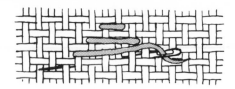

DIAGRAM 9

Lazy daisy stitch and chain stitch (*Diagram 10*) are handy for special effects. Both are worked in the same manner as on regular embroidery.

Lazy Daisy Stitch

Chain Stitch

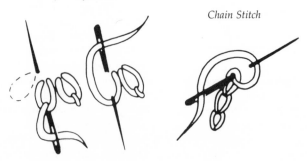

DIAGRAM 10

Embroidery on Linen. Working on linen requires a slightly different technique. While evenweave linen is remarkably regular, there are always a few thick or thin threads. To keep the stitches even, cross-stitch is worked over two threads in each direction (*Diagram 11*).

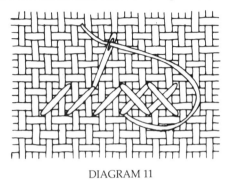

DIAGRAM 11

As you are working over more threads, linen affords a greater variation in stitches. A half-stitch can slant in either direction and is uncrossed. A three-quarters stitch is shown in *Diagram 12*.

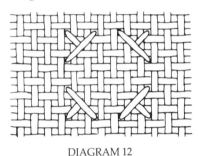

DIAGRAM 12

Diagram 13 shows the backstitch worked on linen.

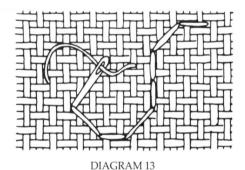

DIAGRAM 13

Embroidery on Gingham. Gingham and other checked fabrics can be used for cross-stitch. Using the fabric as a guide, work the stitches from corner to corner of each check.

Embroidery on Uneven-Weave Fabrics. If you wish to work cross-stitch on an uneven-weave fabric, baste a lightweight Penelope needlepoint canvas to the material. The design can then be stitched by working the cross-stitch over the double mesh of the canvas. When working in this manner, take care not to catch the threads of the canvas in the embroidery. After the cross-stitch is completed, remove the basting threads. With tweezers remove first the vertical threads, one strand at a time, of the needlepoint canvas, then the horizontal threads.

NEEDLEPOINT

One of the most common methods for working needlepoint is from a charted design. By simply viewing each square of a chart as a stitch on the canvas, the patterns quickly and easily translate from one technique to another.

MATERIALS

1. **Needles.** A blunt tapestry needle with a rounded tip and an elongated eye. The needle must clear the hole of the canvas without spreading the threads. For No. 10 canvas, a No. 18 needle works best.

2. **Canvas.** There are two distinct types of needlepoint canvas: single-mesh (mono canvas) and double-mesh (Penelope canvas). Single-mesh canvas, the more common of the two, is easier on the eyes as the spaces are slightly larger. Double-mesh canvas has two horizontal and two vertical threads forming each mesh. The latter is a very stable canvas on which the threads stay securely in place as the work progresses. Canvas is available in many sizes, from 5 mesh-per-inch to 18 mesh-per-inch, and even smaller. The number of mesh-per-inch will, of course, determine the dimensions of the finished needlepoint project. A 60 square × 120 square chart will measure 12″ × 24″ on 5 mesh-to-the-inch canvas, 5″ × 10″ on 12 mesh-to-the-inch canvas. The most common canvas size is 10 to the inch.

3. **Yarns.** Persian, crewel and tapestry yarns all work well on needlepoint canvas.

PREPARING TO WORK

Allow 1″ to 1½″ blank canvas all around. Bind the raw edges of the canvas with masking tape or machine-stitched double-fold bias tape.

There are few hard-and-fast rules on where to begin the design. It is best to complete the main motif, then fill the background as the last step.

For any guidelines you wish to draw on the canvas, take care that your marking medium is waterproof. Nonsoluble inks, acrylic paints thinned with water so as not to clog the mesh, and waterproof felt-tip pens all work well. If unsure, experiment on a scrap of canvas.

When working with multiple strands (such as Persian yarn) always separate (strand) the yarn before beginning to stitch. This one small step allows for better coverage of the canvas. When you need more than one piece of yarn in the needle, use separate strands and do not double the yarn. For example: If you need two strands of 3-ply Persian yarn, use two separated strands. Yarn has a nap (just as fabrics do) and can be felt to be smoother in one direction than the other. Always work with the nap (the smooth side) pointing down.

For 5 mesh-to-the-inch canvas, use six strands of 3-ply yarn; for 10 mesh-to-the-inch canvas, use three strands of 3-ply yarn.

STITCHING

Cut yarn lengths 18″ long. Begin needlepoint by holding about 1″ of loose yarn on the wrong side of the work and working the first several stitches over the loose end to secure it. To end a piece of yarn, run it under several completed stitches on the wrong side of the work.

There are hundreds of needlepoint stitch variations, but tent stitch is universally considered to be *the* needlepoint stitch. The most familiar versions of tent stitch are half-cross stitch, continental stitch and basket-weave stitch.

Half-cross stitch (*Diagram 14*) is worked from left to right. The canvas is then turned around and the return row is again stitched from left to right. Holding the needle vertically, bring it to the front of the canvas through the hole that will be the bottom of the first stitch. Keep the stitches loose for minimum distortion and good coverage. Half-cross stitch is best worked on a double-mesh canvas.

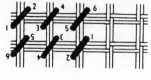

DIAGRAM 14

Continental stitch (*Diagram 15*) begins in the upper right-hand corner and is worked from right to left. The needle is slanted and always brought out a mesh ahead. The resulting stitch appears as a half-cross stitch on the front and as a slanting stitch on the back. When the row is complete, turn the canvas around to work the return row, continuing to stitch from right to left.

DIAGRAM 15

Basket-weave stitch (*Diagram 16*) begins in the upper right-hand corner with four continental stitches (two stitches worked horizontally across the top and two placed directly below the first stitch). Work diagonal rows, the first slanting up and across the canvas from right to left, and the next down and across from left to right. Moving down the canvas from left to right, the needle is in a vertical position; working in the opposite direction, the needle is horizontal. The rows interlock, creating a basket-weave pattern on the wrong side. If the stitch is not done properly, a faint ridge will show where the pattern was interrupted. On basket-weave stitch, always stop working in the middle of a row, rather than at the end, so that you will know in which direction you were working.

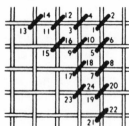

DIAGRAM 16

KNITTING

Charted designs can be worked into stockinette stitch as you are knitting, or they can be embroidered with duplicate stitch when the knitting is complete. For the former, wind the different colors of yarn on bobbins and work in the same manner as in Fair Isle knitting. A few quick Fair Isle tips: (1) Always bring up the new color yarn from under the dropped color to prevent holes. (2) Carry the color not in use loosely across the wrong side of the work, but not more than three or four stitches without twisting the yarns. If a color is not in use for more than seven or eight stitches, it is usually best to drop that color yarn and rejoin a new bobbin when the color is again needed.

CROCHET

There are a number of ways in which charts can be used for crochet. Among them are:

SINGLE CROCHET

Single crochet is often seen worked in multiple colors. When changing colors, always pick up the new color for the last yarn-over of the old color. The color not in use can be carried loosely across the back of the work for a few stitches, or you can work the single crochet over the unused color. The latter method makes for a neater appearance on the wrong side, but sometimes the old color peeks through the stitches. This method can also be applied to half-double crochet and double crochet, but keep in mind that the longer stitches will distort the design.

FILET CROCHET

This technique is nearly always worked from charts and uses only one color thread. The result is a solid-color piece with the design filled in and the background left as an open mesh. Care must be taken in selecting the design, as the longer stitch causes distortion.

AFGHAN CROCHET

The most common method here is cross-stitch worked over the afghan stitch. Complete the afghan crochet project. Then, following the chart for color placement, work cross-stitch over the squares of crochet.

OTHER CHARTED METHODS

Latch hook, Assisi embroidery, beading, cross-stitch on needlepoint canvas (a European favorite) and lace net embroidery are among the other needlework methods worked from charts.

SIX STRAND EMBROIDERY COTTON (FLOSS) CONVERSION CHART

KEY: T = Possible Substitute   * = Close Match   — = No Match

DMC NO.	ROYAL MOULINE NO.	BATES/ANCHOR NO.
White	1001	2
Ecru	8600	926
208	3335*	110*
209	3415*	105
210	3320*	104
211	3410	108*
221	2570	897*
223	2555	894
224	2545	893
225	2540	892
300	8330	352*
301	8315*	349*
304	2415*	47*
307	6005*	289*
309	2525*	42*
310	1002	403
311	4275T	149*
312	—	147*
315	3130	896*
316	3120	895*
317	1030*	400*
318	1020*	399*
319	5025	246*
320	5015	216*
321	2415	47
322	—	978*
326	2530*	59*
327	3365*	101*
333	4250T	119
334	2525T	145
335	4270*	42*
336	5005*	149*
340	—	118
341	—	117
347	2425*	13*
349	2400	13
350	2045T	11
351	2015T	11*
352	2015	10*
353	2010*	8*
355	8095	5968
356	8090	5975*
367	5020	216*
368	5005*	240*
369	5005	213*
370	—	889*
371	—	888*
372	—	887*
400	8325*	351
402	8305*	347*
407	8005*	882*
413	1025*	401
414	1020*	400*
415	1015	398
420	8720*	375*
422	8710*	373*
433	8265	371*
434	8215	309
435	8210*	369*
436	8205	363*

DMC NO.	ROYAL MOULINE NO.	BATES/ANCHOR NO.
437	8200*	362
444	6155*	291
445	6000	288
451	—	399*
452	—	399*
453	1015T	397*
469	5255	267*
470	5255*	267
471	5245	266*
472	5240	264*
498	2425T	20*
500	5125	879*
501	5120*	878
502	5110	876
503	5105	875
504	5100	213*
517	—	169*
518	4860*	168*
519	4855T	167*
520	—	862*
522	—	859*
523	—	859*
524	1115T	858*
535	—	401*
543	8500	933*
550	3380*	102*
552	3370*	101
553	3360	98
554	3355*	96*
561	—	212*
562	—	210*
563	—	208*
564	—	203*
580	5935	267*
581	5925	266*
597	4860*	168*
598	4855*	167*
600	2225*	59*
601	2225*	78*
602	2640*	77*
603	2720*	76*
604	2710	75*
605	2155	50*
606	7260	335
608	7255	333*
610	5825T	889*
611	5735T	898
612	8815*	832
613	5605*	956*
632	8530	936*
640	8625	903
642	8620*	392
644	8800	830
645	1115	905*
646	1115*	8581*
647	1110	8581*
648	1100*	900
666	2405	46
676	6250	891
677	—	886*

DMC NO.	ROYAL MOULINE NO.	BATES/ANCHOR NO.
680	6260*	901
699	5375	923*
700	5365*	229
701	5365*	227
702	5330	239
703	5320	238
704	5310*	256*
712	8600*	387*
718	3015*	88
720	—	326
721	—	324*
722	—	323*
725	6215	306*
726	6150*	295
727	6135	293
729	6255	890
730	—	924*
731	—	281*
732	5925T	281*
733	—	280*
734	—	279*
738	8245*	942
739	8240*	885*
740	7045	316
741	6105	304
742	6120	303
743	6210	297
744	6110*	301*
745	6105	300*
746	6100	386*
747	4850	158*
754	8075	778*
758	8080	868
760	2035	9*
761	2030	8*
762	1010*	397
772	4600*	264*
775	2110*	128*
776	3110	24*
778	—	968*
780	8215*	310*
781	8215	309*
782	6230	308
783	6220*	307
791	4165*	941*
792	4155T	940
793	4155	121*
794	4145	120*
796	4340	133*
797	4265*	132*
798	4325	131*
799	4250*	130*
800	4310	128
801	8405	357*
806	4870T	169*
807	4860*	168*
809	4145*	130*
813	4610*	160*
814	2340T	44*
815	2530*	43

DMC NO.	ROYAL MOULINE NO.	BATES/ANCHOR NO.
816	2530	44*
817	2415T	19
818	2505*	48
819	2000	892*
820	4345	134
822	8605*	387*
823	4400*	150
824	4225	164*
825	4215	162*
826	4210	161*
827	4605	159*
828	4850	158*
829	5825	906
830	5825*	889*
831	5825T	889*
832	5815	907
833	5815*	874*
834	5810*	874
838	8425*	380
839	8560	380*
840	8555	379*
841	8550	378*
842	8505	376*
844	1115T	401*
869	8720*	944*
890	5025*	879*
891	2135	35*
892	2130	28
893	2125*	27
894	2115T	26
895	5430*	246*
898	8425*	360
899	2515	27*
900	7230*	333
902	—	72*
904	5295*	258*
905	5295*	258*
906	5285*	256*
907	5280*	255
909	5370	229*
910	5370*	228*
911	5465*	205*
912	5465	205
913	5460*	209
915	3030	89*
917	3020*	89*
918	8330*	341*
919	8095*	341*
920	8060*	339*
921	8060T	349*
922	8315T	324*
924	4830T	851*
926	4820*	779*
927	4810T	849*
928	1010T	900*
930	4510	922*
931	4505	921*
932	4500	920*
934	5070T	862*
935	5225T	862*

DMC NO.	ROYAL MOULINE NO.	BATES/ANCHOR NO.
936	5260T	269
937	5260	268
938	8430	381
939	4405	127
943	4935*	188*
945	8020*	347*
946	7230*	332*
947	7255*	330*
948	8070	778*
950	8020T	4146
951	8020T	366*
954	5455*	203*
955	5450	206*
956	2170*	40*
957	2160T	40*
958	—	187
959	—	186
961	2515*	76*
962	2515	76*
963	2505	49*
964	—	185
966	5150*	214*
970	7040	316*
971	7045	316*
972	6120*	298
973	6015	290
975	8365	355*
976	8355	308*
977	8350	307*
986	5430	246*
987	5020T	244*
988	5295T	243*
989	5405T	242*
991	5165T	189*
992	4925*	187*
993	4915*	186*
995	4710	410
996	4700	433
3011	5525T	845*
3012	5525*	844*
3013	5515	842*
3021	—	382*
3022	—	8581*
3023	—	8581*
3024	1100	900*
3031	—	905*
3032	8620T	903*
3033	8610*	388*
3041	3215*	871
3045	3205*	869
3046	6260T	373*
3047	5810	887*
3051	5805	886*
3052	5530T	846*
3053	5060*	859*
3064	5055*	859*
3072	8005*	914*
3078	4805*	397*
—	6130	292*
3325	4200	159*

DMC NO.	ROYAL MOULINE NO.	BATES/ANCHOR NO.
3326	2115*	25*
3328	2045	11*
3340	—	329
3341	—	328
3345	5025T	268*
3346	5220T	257*
3347	5210*	266*
3348	5270*	265
3350	2220	42*
3354	2210	74*
3362	—	862*
3363	—	861*
3364	—	843*
3371	8435	382
3607	—	87*
3608	—	86
3609	—	85
3685	2335	70*
3687	2325	69*
3688	2320	66*
3689	2310	49
3705	—	35*
3706	—	28*
3708	—	26*
48	9000*	1201*
51	9014	1220
52	9006	1208
53	—	
57	9002	1203
61	9013T	1218*
62	9000T	1201*
67	—	1211*
69	—	1216*
75	9002	1206*
90	9012T	1217*
91	9008*	1211
92	9007*	1216*
93	9007*	1210*
94	9011*	1216
95	9006T	1208*
99	9005T	1207*
101	9009*	1213*
102	—	1208*
103	—	1210*
104	9012	1217
105	9013*	1218*
106	9002T	1203*
107	9003	1204
108	9014*	1220*
111	9003T	1204*
112	9007*	1210*
113	—	1208*
114	9010	1215
115	9004	1206
121	9007	1210
122	9010T	1215*
123	—	1213*
124	9007T	1210*
125	9009	1213
126	9006*	1208*

floral garland zodiac

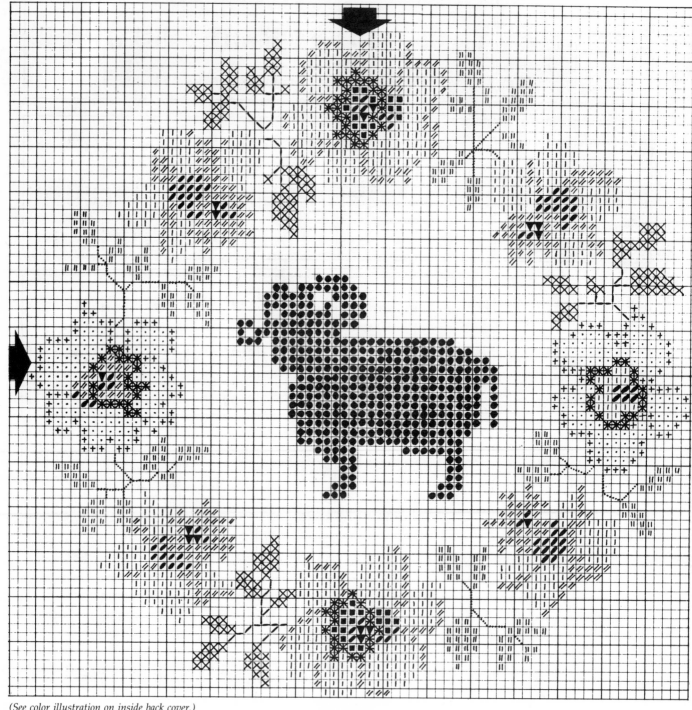

(See color illustration on inside back cover.)

ARIES
march 21–april 20

DMC #

⊞	415	Pearl Gray		▣	970	Light Pumpkin
⊡	973	Bright Canary		⊙	895	Dark Christmas Green
⊠	904	Very Dark Parrot Green		◪	972	Deep Canary
⌐-⌐	904	Very Dark Parrot Green (backstitch)		◩	783	Christmas Gold
⫼	907	Light Parrot Green		▼	434	Light Brown
⋯	907	Light Parrot Green (backstitch)		✳	946	Medium Burnt Orange
⊡		White				

8

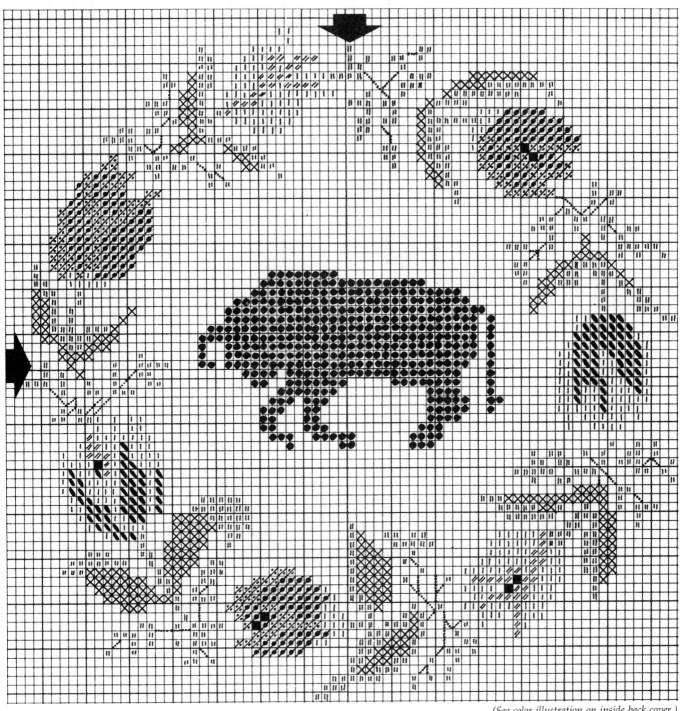

(See color illustration on inside back cover.)

taurus

april 21–may 20

DMC #

⊞	973	Bright Canary
⊠	904	Very Dark Parrot Green
⫼	907	Light Parrot Green
⋯⋅⋅⫶	907	Light Parrot Green (backstitch)
■		Black

◉	895	Dark Christmas Green
⧄	972	Deep Canary
◥	606	Bright Orange Red
⊡	603	Cranberry
⧄	891	Dark Carnation

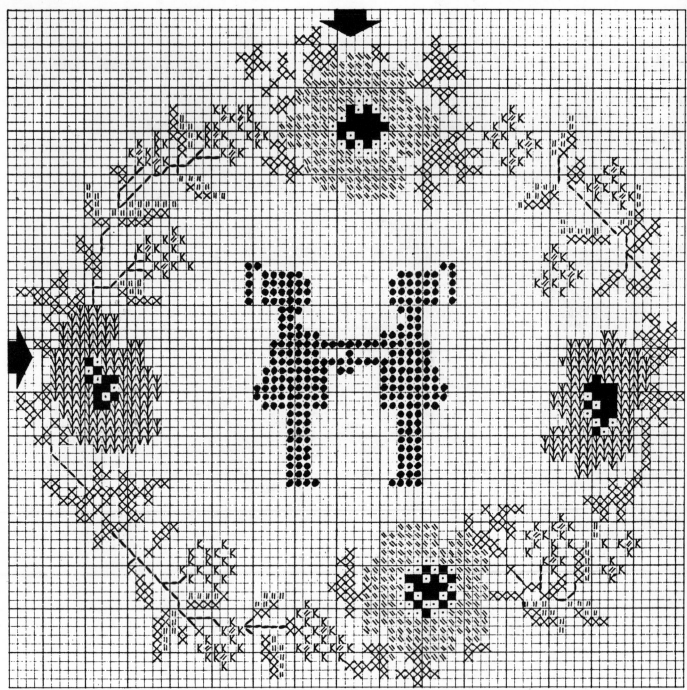

(See color illustration on inside back cover.)

Gemini

may 21–june 21

DMC #

☒	904	Very Dark Parrot Green		⊡	895	Dark Christmas Green
- -◞	904	Very Dark Parrot Green (backstitch)		☒	553	Medium Violet
⫼	907	Light Parrot Green		☒	972	Deep Canary
⊡		White		☒	893	Light Carnation
▪		Black		☒	334	Medium Bay Blue

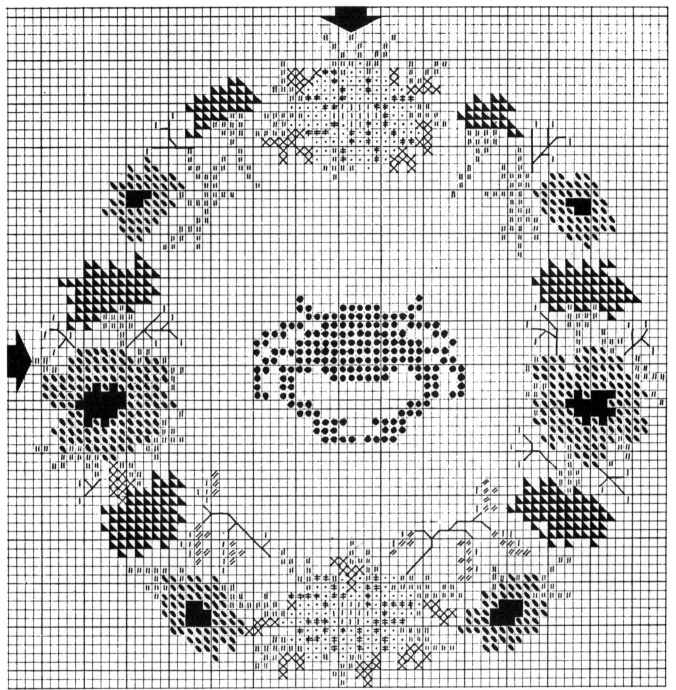

(See color illustration on inside back cover.)

CANCER

June 22–July 22

DMC #

🔅	762	Very Light Pearl Gray
Ⅱ	973	Bright Canary
╱	973	Bright Canary (backstitch)
⊠	904	Very Dark Parrot Green
Ⅲ	907	Light Parrot Green
·		White
◼		Black
⊙	895	Dark Christmas Green
⧄	972	Deep Canary
◥	606	Bright Orange Red
◢	797	Royal Blue

(See color illustration on inside back cover.)

leo

july 23–august 22

	DMC #				
⊥	973	Bright Canary	◉	895	Dark Christmas Green
☒	904	Very Dark Parrot Green	◤	718	Plum
_ _ ⁻ ⁻	904	Very Dark Parrot Green (backstitch)	ⱴ	553	Medium Violet
Ⅲ	907	Light Parrot Green	⊙	552	Dark Violet
■		Black	⧄	972	Deep Canary

(See color illustration on inside back cover.)

VIRGO

august 23–septemBeR 23

DMC #

⊡	973	Bright Canary
⊠	904	Very Dark Parrot Green
⌐⁄⁻	904	Very Dark Parrot Green (backstitch)
⫼	907	Light Parrot Green
◉	895	Dark Christmas Green
◎	552	Dark Violet
◥	893	Light Carnation

◣	606	Bright Orange Red
◪	3685	Dark Mauve
▨	603	Cranberry
▲	917	Medium Rose
◪	891	Dark Carnation
∿	895	Dark Christmas Green (backstitch)

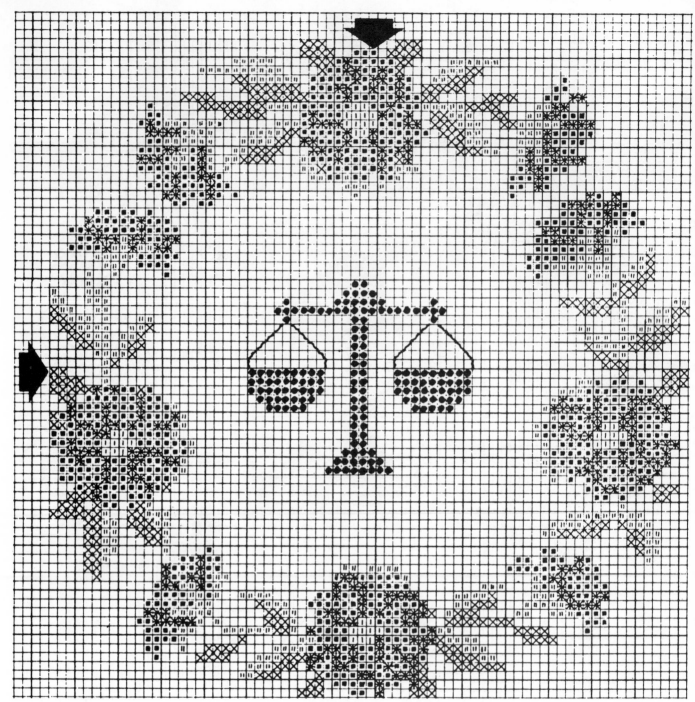

(See color illustration on inside back cover.)

LIBRA

SEPTEMBER 24–OCTOBER 23

DMC #

⊞	973	Bright Canary	⊡	895	Dark Christmas Green
⊠	904	Very Dark Parrot Green	⌣	895	Dark Christmas Green (backstitch)
⊞	907	Light Parrot Green	✳	946	Medium Burnt Orange
▣	970	Light Pumpkin			

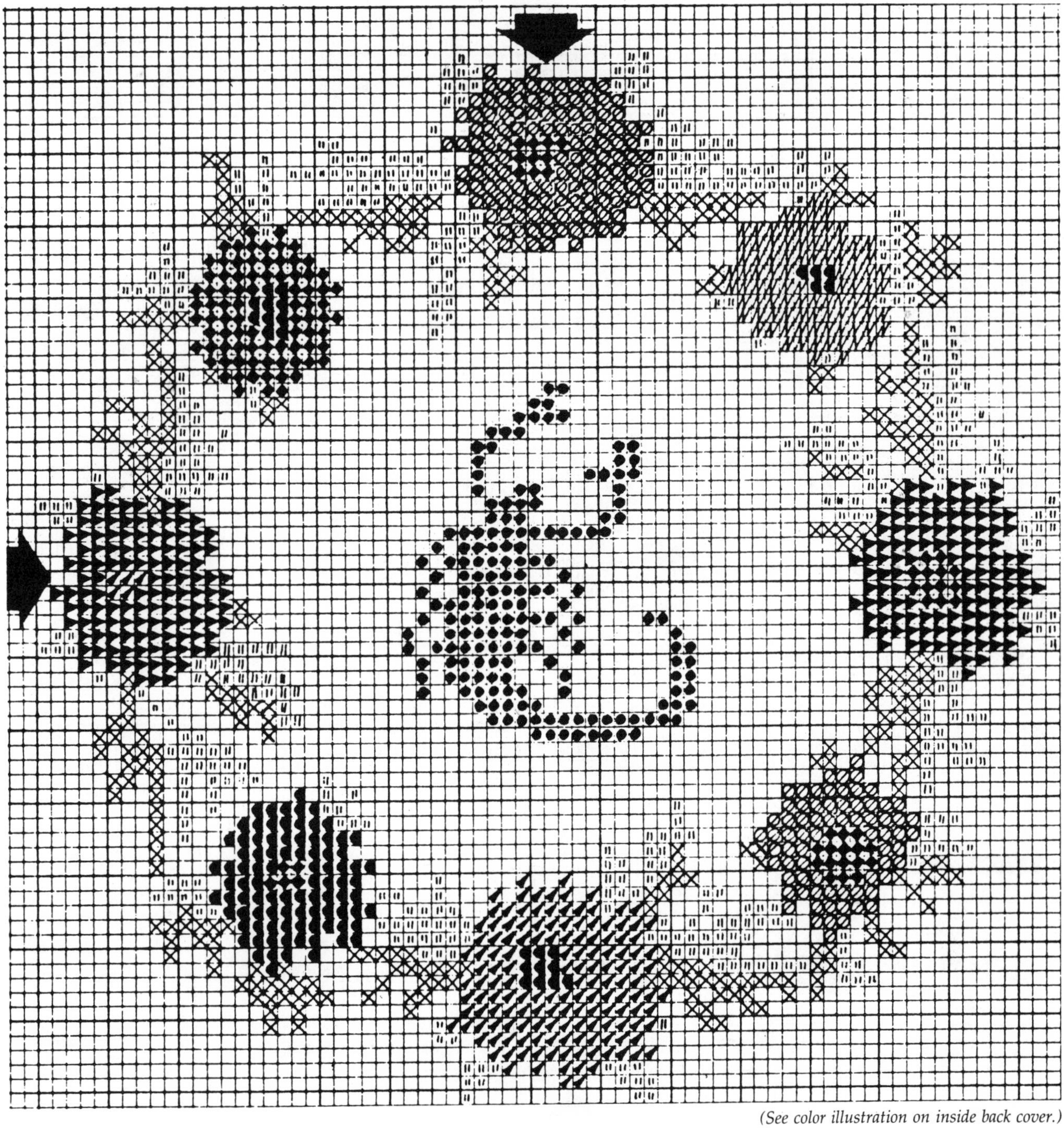

(See color illustration on inside back cover.)

SCORPIO

OCTOBER 24–NOVEMBER 21

	DMC #	
☒	904	Very Dark Parrot Green
⊞	907	Light Parrot Green
●	895	Dark Christmas Green
◩	718	Plum
◖	3685	Dark Mauve
▶	915	Dark Plum
⊘	349	Dark Coral
◆	498	Dark Christmas Red
Ⓝ	347	Dark Salmon

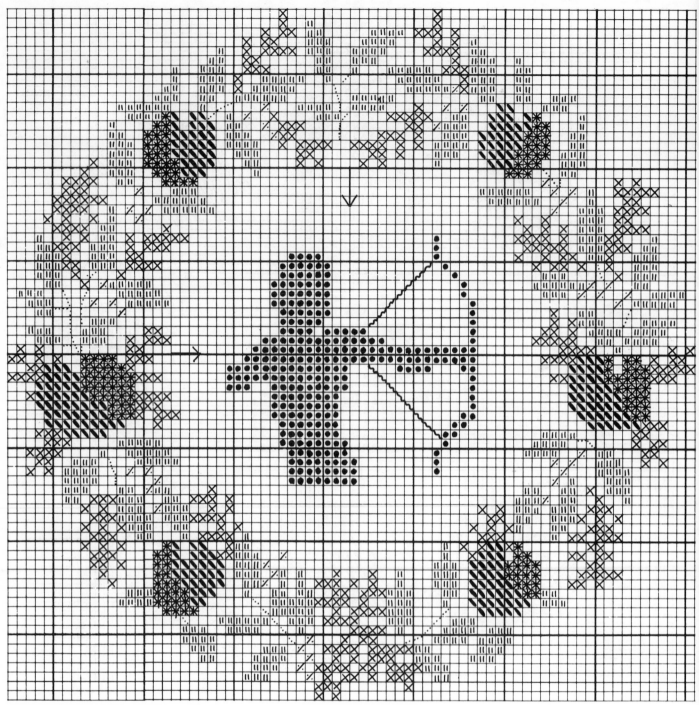

(See color illustration on inside back cover.)

SAGITTARIUS

NOVEMBER 22–DECEMBER 21

DMC #

⊠	904	Very Dark Parrot Green	∿	895	Dark Christmas Green (backstitch)
Ⅲ	907	Light Parrot Green	✳	946	Medium Burnt Orange
⋯	907	Light Parrot Green (backstitch)	◣	606	Bright Orange Red
◉	895	Dark Christmas Green	⊡	603	Cranberry

(See color illustration on inside back cover.)

CAPRICORN
December 22–January 20

DMC #

☒	904	Very Dark Parrot Green	◨	606	Bright Orange Red
◫	907	Light Parrot Green	⌐	907	Light Parrot Green
◉	895	Dark Christmas Green			(backstitch)
▨	972	Deep Canary			

(See color illustration on inside back cover.)

aquarius

JANUARY 21–fEBRUARY 18

DMC #

⊡	415	Pearl Gray
Ⅱ	973	Bright Canary
☒	904	Very Dark Parrot Green
⌐⌐	904	Very Dark Parrot Green (backstitch)

⫼	907	Light Parrot Green
·		White
■	970	Light Pumpkin
◉	895	Dark Christmas Green

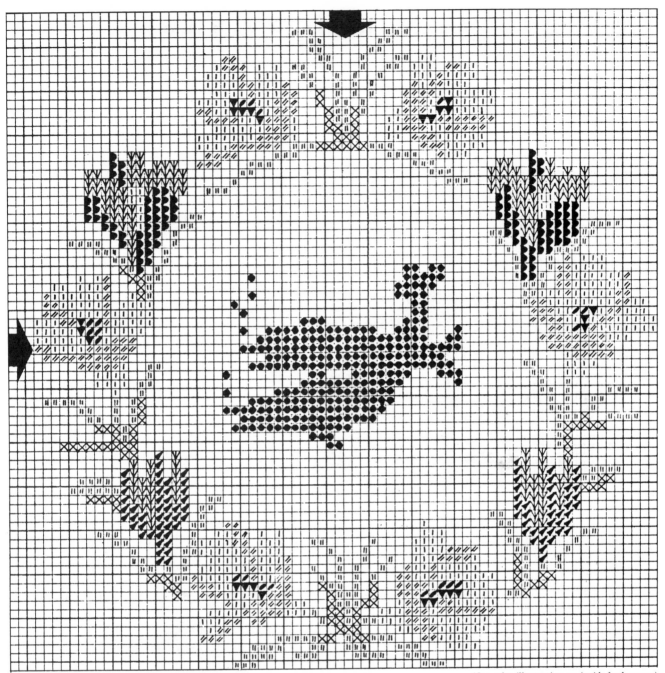

(See color illustration on inside back cover.)

pisces

february 19–march 20

DMC #

⊞	973	Bright Canary		◩	553	Medium Violet
☒	904	Very Dark Parrot Green		◪	972	Deep Canary
Ⅱ	907	Light Parrot Green		◪	783	Christmas Gold
◐	895	Dark Christmas Green		▼	434	Light Brown
◩	718	Plum		◗	550	Very Dark Violet

flower-circled zodiac

Note: Chart for border appears on Pisces design, page 24.

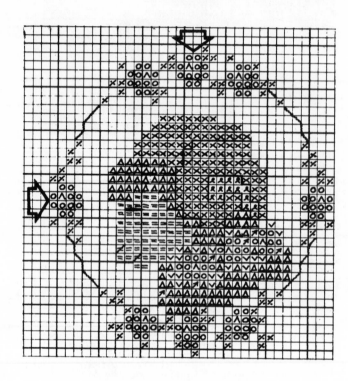

ARIES

march 21–april 20

	DMC #	
⊟	642	Dark Beige Gray
◭	646	Dark Beaver Gray
✕	420	Dark Hazelnut Brown
⅃	433	Medium Brown
—	433	Medium Brown (backstitch)
▽	906	Medium Parrot Green
↗	519	Sky Blue
⊙	604	Light Cranberry
◬	600	Very Dark Cranberry
～	600	Very Dark Cranberry (backstitch)
☒	469	Avocado Green
	519	Sky Blue (border)

TAURUS

april 21–may 20

	DMC #	
◪	780	Very Dark Topaz
⅃	433	Medium Brown
·	945	Flesh
▨	444	Dark Lemon
⊟	642	Dark Beige Gray
◭	646	Dark Beaver Gray
●		Black
—	433	Medium Brown (backstitch)
⊙	604	Light Cranberry
☒	469	Avocado Green
◬	600	Very Dark Cranberry
～	600	Very Dark Cranberry (backstitch)
		Black (backstitch around eyes)
⊂		White
	604	Light Cranberry (border)

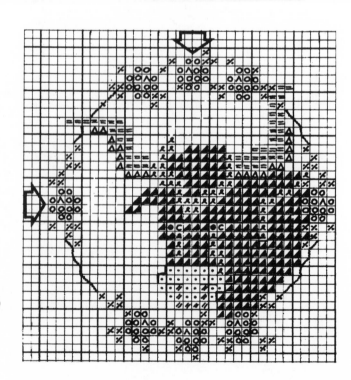

GEMINI

may 21–june 21

DMC #

·	945	Flesh
O	604	Light Cranberry
V	906	Medium Parrot Green
⧄	444	Dark Lemon
—	780	Very Dark Topaz (backstitch)
↗	519	Sky Blue
⧅	469	Avocado Green
3	797	Royal Blue
Λ	600	Very Dark Cranberry
∿∿	600	Very Dark Cranberry (backstitch)
	519	Sky Blue (border)

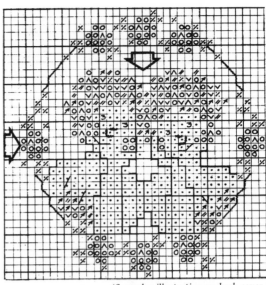

(See color illustration on back cover.)

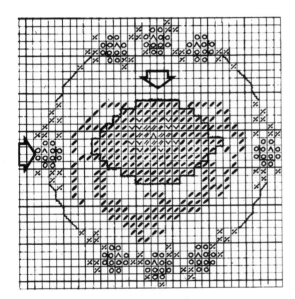

CANCER

june 22–july 22

DMC #

⧄	3326	Light Rose
V	906	Medium Parrot Green
⧄	444	Dark Lemon
O	604	Light Cranberry
⧅	469	Avocado Green
Λ	600	Very Dark Cranberry
∿∿	600	Very Dark Cranberry (backstitch)
	604	Light Cranberry (border)

LEO

july 23–august 22

DMC #

Z	783	Christmas Gold
◣	780	Very Dark Topaz
	444	Dark Lemon (straight stitch for eyes)
—	433	Medium Brown (backstitch for nose)
—		Black (backstitch for eyes and mouth)
O	604	Light Cranberry
⧅	469	Avocado Green
Λ	600	Very Dark Cranberry
∿∿	600	Very Dark Cranberry (backstitch)
	519	Sky Blue (border)

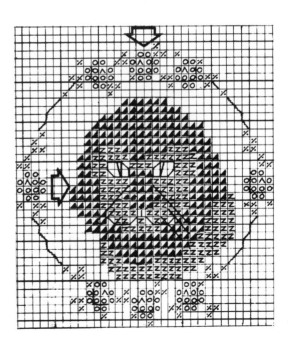

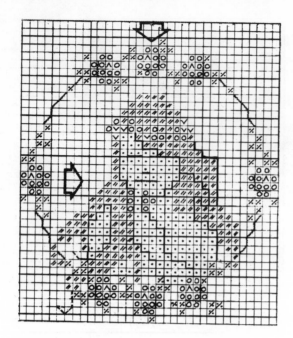

VIRGO

august 23–september 23

DMC #

·	945	Flesh
⊘	444	Dark Lemon
Ⓥ	906	Medium Parrot Green
--'--	444	Dark Lemon (backstitch)
—	780	Very Dark Topaz (backstitch)
—	995	Dark Electric Blue (backstitch for eyes)
⋀	600	Very Dark Cranberry
⌇	600	Very Dark Cranberry (backstitch)
Ⓞ	604	Light Cranberry
⊠	469	Avocado Green
	604	Light Cranberry (border)

LIBRA

september 24–october 23

DMC #

◿	995	Dark Electric Blue
Ⓣ	606	Bright Orange Red
Ⓥ	906	Medium Parrot Green
⊘	444	Dark Lemon
—	433	Medium Brown (backstitch)
⊠	469	Avocado Green
Ⓞ	604	Light Cranberry
⋀	600	Very Dark Cranberry
⌇	600	Very Dark Cranberry (backstitch)
	519	Sky Blue (border)

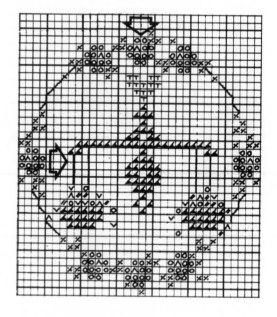

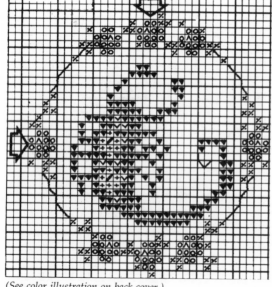

SCORPIO

october 24–november 21

DMC #

▼	917	Medium Plum
—	917	Medium Plum (backstitch)
⊞	947	Burnt Orange
Ⓥ	906	Medium Parrot Green
Ⓞ	604	Light Cranberry
⊠	469	Avocado Green
◣	444	Dark Lemon
⋀	600	Very Dark Cranberry
⌇	600	Very Dark Cranberry (backstitch)
	604	Light Cranberry (border)

(See color illustration on back cover.)

SAGITTARIUS

NOVEMBER 22–DECEMBER 21

DMC #

⊡	945	Flesh
🗼	433	Medium Brown
--⌐--	433	Medium Brown (backstitch)
▨	469	Avocado Green
—	469	Avocado Green (backstitch)
▣	604	Light Cranberry
◭	600	Very Dark Cranberry
∼∼∼	600	Very Dark Cranberry (backstitch)
	519	Sky Blue (border)

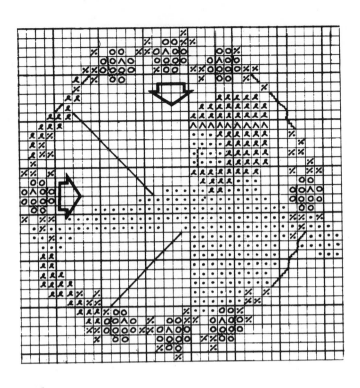

CAPRICORN

DECEMBER 22–JANUARY 20

DMC #

⬚	318	Light Steel Gray
△	646	Dark Beaver Gray
⊠	420	Dark Hazelnut Brown
●		Black
—		Black (backstitch)
▣	604	Light Cranberry
▨	469	Avocado Green
◭	600	Very Dark Cranberry
∼∼∼	600	Very Dark Cranberry (backstitch)
	604	Light Cranberry (border)

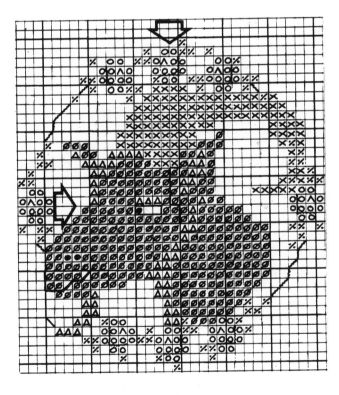

Note: Chart for border appears on Pisces design, page 24.

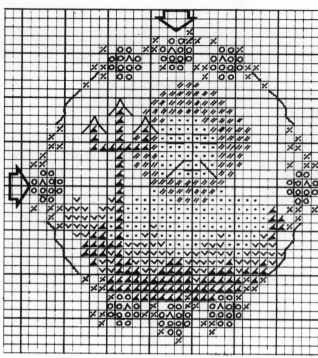

aquarius

january 21–february 18

DMC #

⊘	444	Dark Lemon
⊡	945	Flesh
—	780	Very Dark Topaz (backstitch)
▽	906	Medium Parrot Green
⊿	995	Dark Electric Blue
⊙	604	Light Cranberry
⊠	469	Avocado Green
◿	600	Very Dark Cranberry
∿∿∿	600	Very Dark Cranberry (backstitch)
	519	Sky Blue (border)

(See color illustration on front cover.)

pisces

february 19–march 20

DMC #

⊿	995	Dark Electric Blue
▽	906	Medium Parrot Green
⊘	444	Dark Lemon
◿	600	Very Dark Cranberry
∿∿∿	600	Very Dark Cranberry (backstitch)
⊙	604	Light Cranberry
⊠	469	Avocado Green
	604	Light Cranberry (border)

COLOR KEY FOR BORDER

⊙		Border as indicated on each Color Key
⊠	469	Avocado Green
●	604	Light Cranberry
▲	600	Very Dark Cranberry

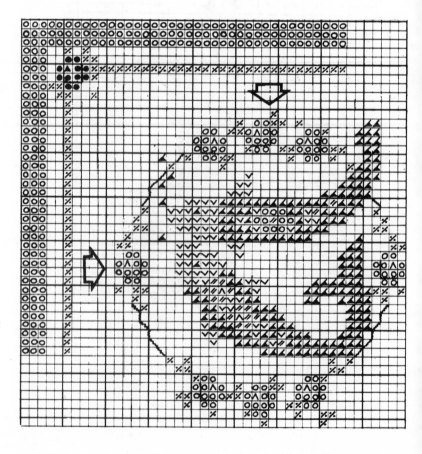

fanciful zodiac

ARIES

march 21–april 20

DMC #

●		Black
—		Black (backstitch on ram)
·		White
V		Silver
—		Silver (backstitch on star)
◩	611	Dark Drab Brown
▼	434	Light Brown
◪	602	Medium Cranberry
—	602	Medium Cranberry (backstitch on tree trunk)
⊡	604	Light Cranberry
∅	973	Bright Canary
⊘	996	Medium Electric Blue
C	453	Light Shell Gray
◿	3013	Light Khaki Green
⊠	704	Bright Chartreuse

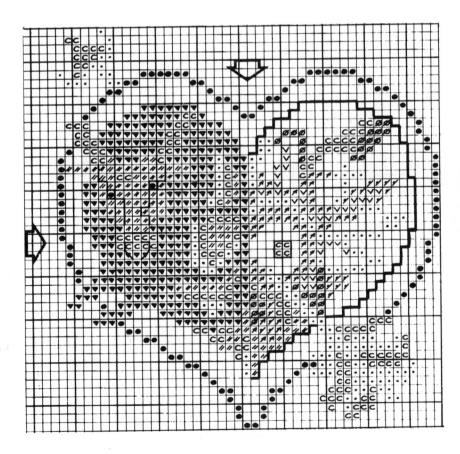

TAURUS

april 21–may 20

DMC #

V		Silver
●		Black
—		Black (backstitch)
▼	938	Ultra Dark Coffee Brown
⊘	434	Light Brown
C	977	Light Golden Brown
·	973	Bright Canary
↗	992	Aquamarine
◩	926	Dark Gray Blue
∅	891	Dark Carnation

GEMINI

MAY 21–JUNE 21

DMC #

◉		Black
∿∿∿		Black (backstitch)
▼	552	Dark Violet
·		White
∨		Silver
—		Silver (backstitch on star)
⊘	973	Bright Canary
3	977	Light Golden Brown
C	818	Baby Pink
⊘	604	Light Cranberry
—	604	Light Cranberry (backstitch skirt outline)
⊘	891	Dark Carnation
━	891	Dark Carnation (backstitch)
6	926	Dark Gray Blue
+++	926	Dark Gray Blue (backstitch)

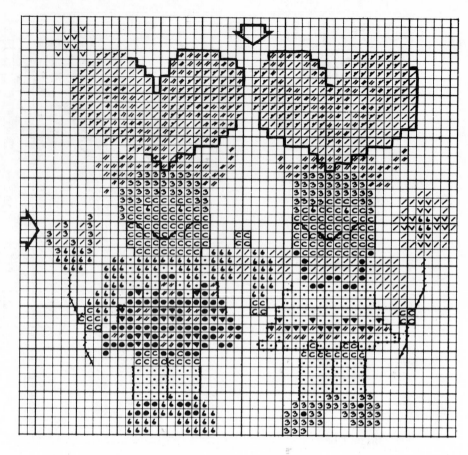

CANCER

JUNE 22–JULY 22

DMC #

⊘	725	Topaz
Y	977	Light Golden Brown
⊘	434	Light Brown
⊘	891	Dark Carnation
C	818	Baby Pink
◣	611	Dark Drab Brown
⊘	733	Medium Olive Green
↗	471	Very Light Avocado Green
▼	646	Dark Beaver Gray
·		White
◉		Black
—		Black (backstitch)
∨		Silver
∿∿∿		Silver (backstitch)

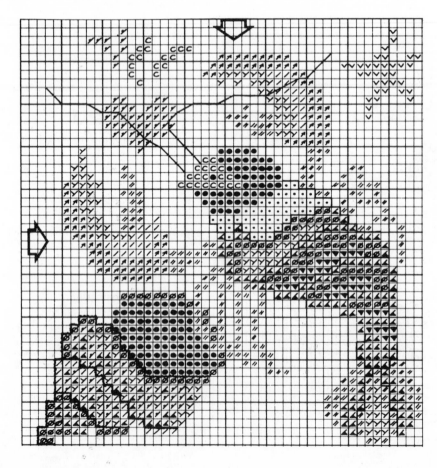

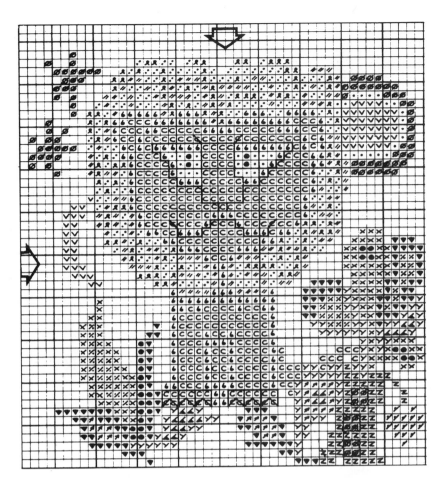

Leo

july 23–august 22

DMC #

6	975	Dark Golden Brown
C	977	Light Golden Brown
▼	469	Avocado Green
X	471	Very Light Avocado Green
↗	472	Ultra Light Avocado Green
Y	704	Bright Chartreuse
Ø	973	Bright Canary
Y	891	Dark Carnation
⊠	602	Medium Canary
⊼	970	Light Pumpkin
◺	926	Dark Gray Blue
Z	646	Dark Beaver Gray
⊠	597	Turquoise
●	995	Dark Electric Blue
·		White
V		Silver
∴	725	Topaz
——		Black (backstitch)

VIRGO

august 23–september 23

DMC #

⊘	725	Topaz
——	725	Topaz (backstitch on flower)
⊠	970	Light Pumpkin
⊡	818	Baby Pink
⊘	604	Light Cranberry
——	604	Light Cranberry (backstitch on arms and face outline)
⊼	602	Medium Cranberry
++	602	Medium Cranberry (backstitch on cheeks)
⊘	891	Dark Carnation
6	926	Dark Gray Blue
↗	597	Turquoise
●		Black
——		Black (backstitch)
V		Silver
——		Silver (backstitch on star)

LIBRA

september 24–october 23

DMC

◹	472	Ultra Light Avocado Green
◤	995	Dark Electric Blue
C	604	Light Cranberry
◿	891	Dark Carnation
◿	453	Light Shell Gray
Z	646	Dark Beaver Gray
3	975	Dark Golden Brown
·		White
●		Black
—		Black (backstitch)
V		Silver
••••		Silver (backstitch on star)
◣	970	Light Pumpkin
··	725	Topaz

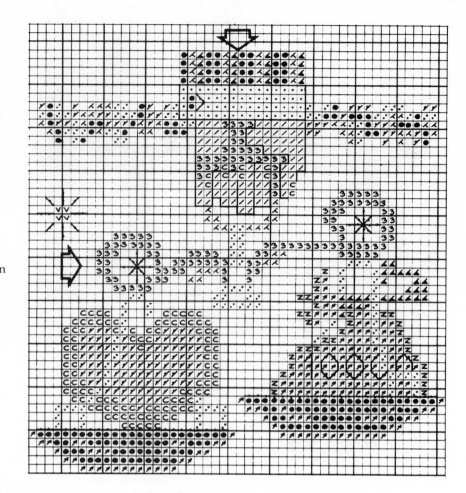

(See color illustration on front cover.)

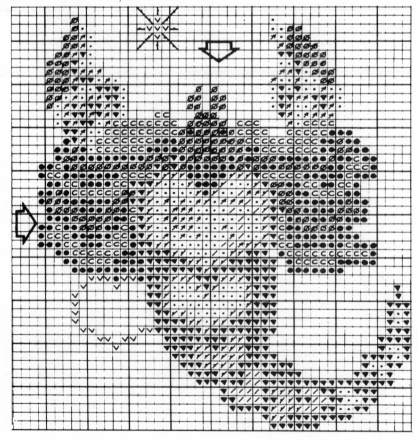

SCORPIO

october 24–november 21

DMC

●		Black
—		Black (backstitch)
V		Silver
••••		Silver (backstitch)
◿	725	Topaz
Ø	733	Medium Olive Green
▼	646	Dark Beaver Gray
C	453	Light Shell Gray
◿	519	Sky Blue
·	604	Light Cranberry
◿	891	Dark Carnation

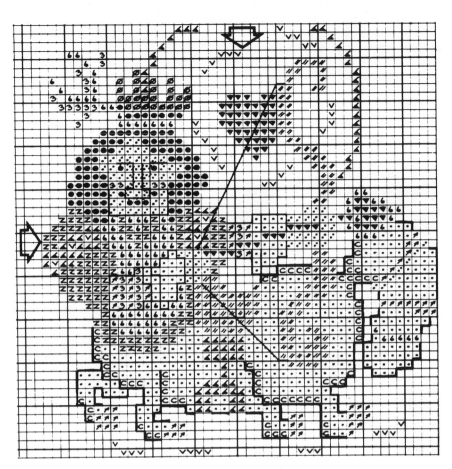

SAGITTARIUS

NOVEMBER 22–DECEMBER 21

DMC #

Symbol	DMC #	Color
·		White
●		Black
—		Black (backstitch)
V		Silver
↗	519	Sky Blue
∅	725	Topaz
·	818	Baby Pink
3	604	Light Cranberry
—	604	Light Cranberry (backstitch on face)
▼	891	Dark Carnation
Z	472	Ultra Light Avocado Green
◢	646	Dark Beaver Gray
—	646	Dark Beaver Gray (backstitch)
C	453	Light Shell Gray
6	552	Dark Violet
⊘	434	Light Brown

(See color illustration on back cover.)

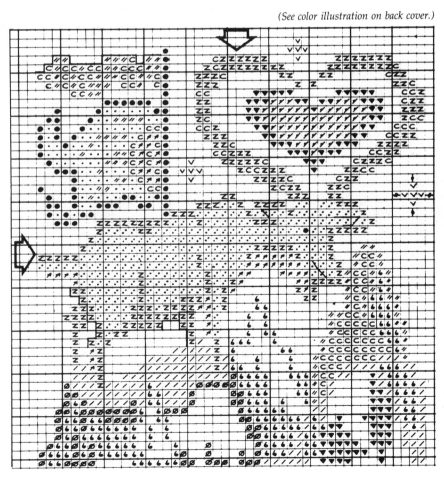

CAPRICORN

DECEMBER 22–JANUARY 20

DMC #

Symbol	DMC #	Color
⊿	471	Very Light Avocado
▼	469	Avocado Green
C	519	Sky Blue
⊘	996	Medium Electric Blue
●		Black
—		Black (backstitch)
·		White
V		Silver
•–•–		Silver (backstitch)
⊻	891	Dark Carnation
↗	604	Light Cranberry
Z	646	Dark Beaver Gray
6	926	Dark Gray Blue
·	453	Light Shell Gray
∅	975	Dark Golden Brown

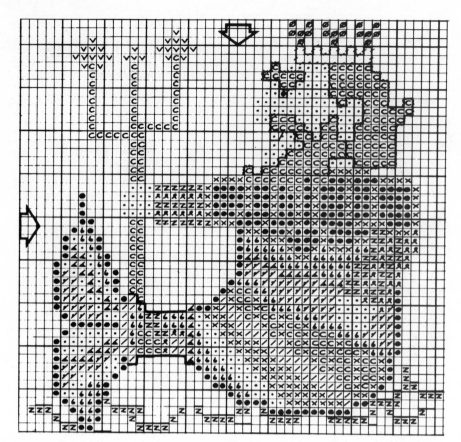

aquarius

january 21–february 18

DMC #

◢	926	Dark Gray Blue
🏃	602	Medium Cranberry
—	602	Medium Cranberry (backstitch for mouth)
Z	996	Medium Electric Blue
◹	519	Sky Blue
◸	469	Avocado Green
X	471	Very Light Avocado Green
·	472	Ultra Light Avocado Green
◣	646	Dark Beaver Gray
～	646	Dark Beaver Gray (backstitch on hair and beard)
C	453	Light Shell Gray
Ø	977	Light Golden Brown
+++	977	Light Golden Brown (backstitch)
⦿		Black
—		Black (backstitch)
V		Silver
—		Silver (backstitch)

pisces

february 19–march 20

DMC #

Ø	597	Turquoise
🏃	926	Dark Gray Blue
◢	970	Light Pumpkin
·	973	Bright Canary
3	725	Topaz
◣	995	Dark Electric Blue
C	996	Medium Electric Blue
Z	646	Dark Beaver Gray
⌀	602	Medium Cranberry
◹	891	Dark Carnation
—	891	Dark Carnation (backstitch for mouth and center line on shell)
V	704	Bright Chartreuse
◥	471	Very Light Avocado Green
⦿		Black
—		Black (backstitch)
+++		Silver (backstitch for bubbles)

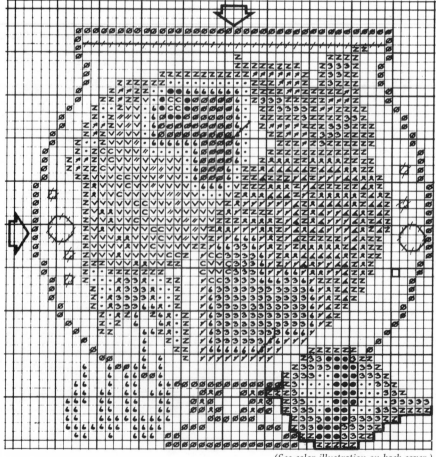

(See color illustration on back cover.)

pROfile ZOdiac

ARIES

MARCH 21–APRIL 20

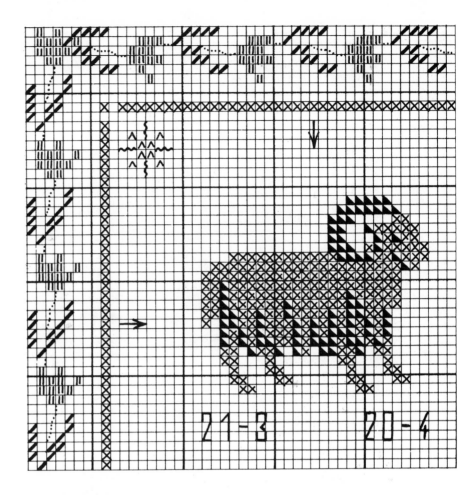

21–3   20–4

DMC

▟	906	Medium Parrot Green
⋯⋯	906	Medium Parrot Green (backstitch)
◣	792	Dark Cornflower Blue
—	792	Dark Cornflower Blue (backstitch)
⊠	798	Dark Delft
◰	972	Deep Canary
∿∿	972	Deep Canary (backstitch)
◎	553	Medium Violet
⫿	335	Rose

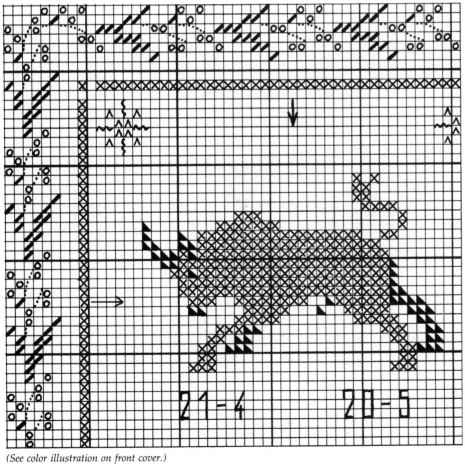

21–4   20–5

TAURUS

APRIL 21–MAY 20

(See color illustration on front cover.)

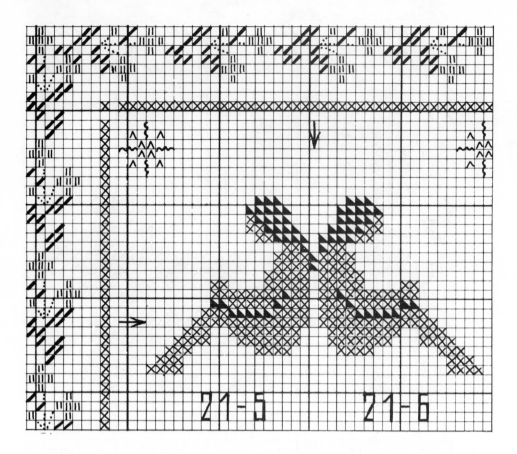

GEMINI
may 21–June 21

DMC #

◪	906	Medium Parrot Green
.....	906	Medium Parrot Green (backstitch)
◪	792	Dark Cornflower Blue
—	792	Dark Cornflower Blue (backstitch)
⊠	798	Dark Delft
Ⲗ	972	Deep Canary
∿∿	972	Deep Canary (backstitch)
Ⅲ	335	Rose

CANCER
June 22–July 22

leo

july 23–august 22

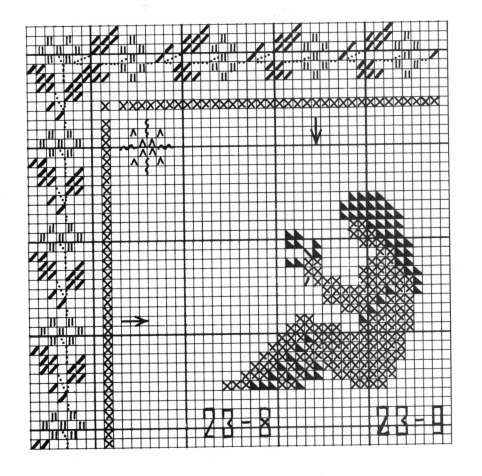

(See color illustration on back cover.)

DMC

◢	906	Medium Parrot Green
·····	906	Medium Parrot Green (backstitch)
◣	792	Dark Cornflower Blue
—	792	Dark Cornflower Blue (backstitch)
⊠	798	Dark Delft
Λ	972	Deep Canary
⌁	972	Deep Canary (backstitch)
◎	553	Medium Violet
‖	335	Rose

VIRGO

august 23–september 23

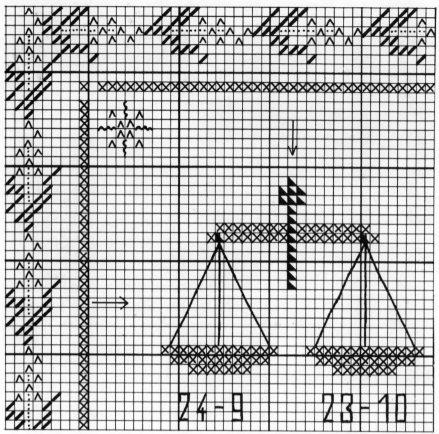

LIBRA
september 24–october 23

(See color illustration on back cover.)

DMC #

◪	906	Medium Parrot Green
·····	906	Medium Parrot Green (backstitch)
◪	792	Dark Cornflower Blue
——	792	Dark Cornflower Blue (backstitch)
⊠	798	Dark Delft
Λ	972	Deep Canary
∿∿∿	972	Deep Canary (backstitch)
⊙	553	Medium Violet

scorpio
october 24–november 21

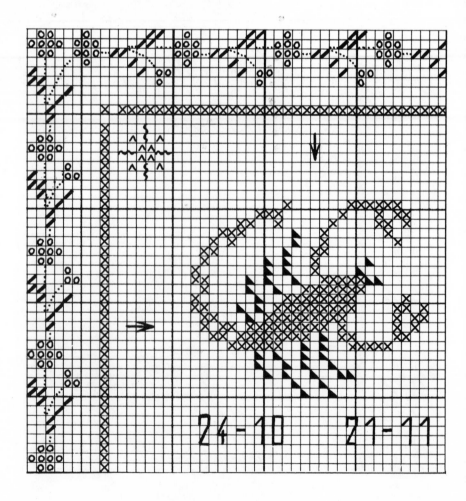

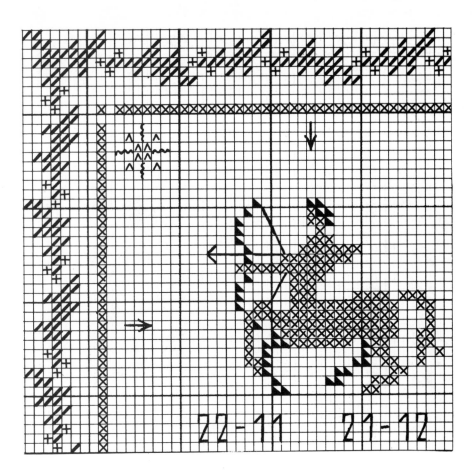

SAGITTARIUS
NOVEMBER 22–DECEMBER 21

	DMC #	
◪	906	Medium Parrot Green
·····	906	Medium Parrot Green (backstitch)
◨	792	Dark Cornflower Blue
—	792	Dark Cornflower Blue (backstitch)
⊠	798	Dark Delft
◿	972	Deep Canary
⌇	972	Deep Canary (backstitch)
⊞	606	Bright Orange Red

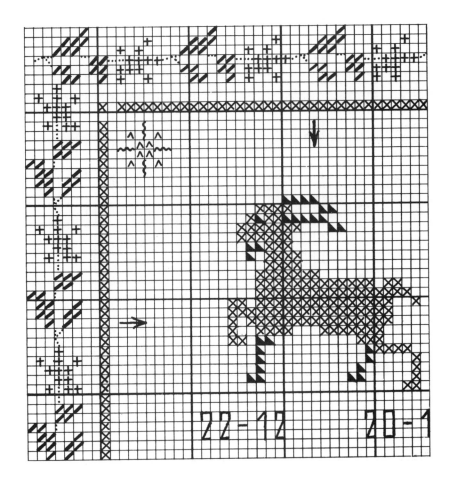

CAPRICORN
DECEMBER 22–JANUARY 20

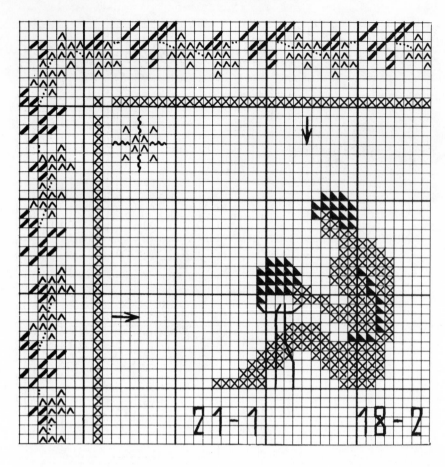

aquarius

January 21–february 18

DMC #

◪	906	Medium Parrot Green
.....	906	Medium Parrot Green (backstitch)
◣	792	Dark Cornflower Blue
—	792	Dark Cornflower Blue (backstitch)
⊠	798	Dark Delft
Λ	972	Deep Canary
⌁	972	Deep Canary (backstitch)
⊡	553	Medium Violet

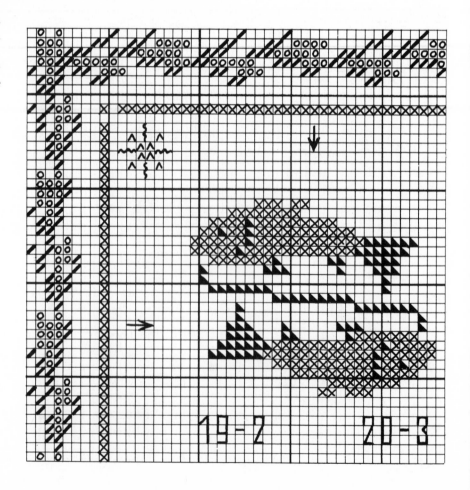

pisces

february 19–march 20

ARBOR ZODIAC

(See color illustration on inside front cover.)

ARIES

MARCH 21–APRIL 20

DMC #

Symbol	#	Color		Symbol	#	Color
X	989	Forest Green		C	334	Medium Bay Blue
⊞	831	Light Avocado Leaf		⬕	642	Dark Beige Gray
X	830	Medium Avocado Leaf		■	368	Light Pistachio Green
⊞	676	Light Old Gold		⬔ {	642	Dark Beige Gray, 1 strand
O	307	Lemon			644	Medium Drab Brown, 2 strands
9	451	Dark Shell Gray				
V	611	Dark Drab Brown				

Symbol	#	Color
·	3033	Very Light Mocha Brown
⬕ {	453	Light Shell Gray, 1 strand
	452	Medium Shell Gray, 2 strands
⊠	612	Medium Drab Brown
−	644	Medium Beige Gray

When a symbol represents two colors, use the two together in the needle.

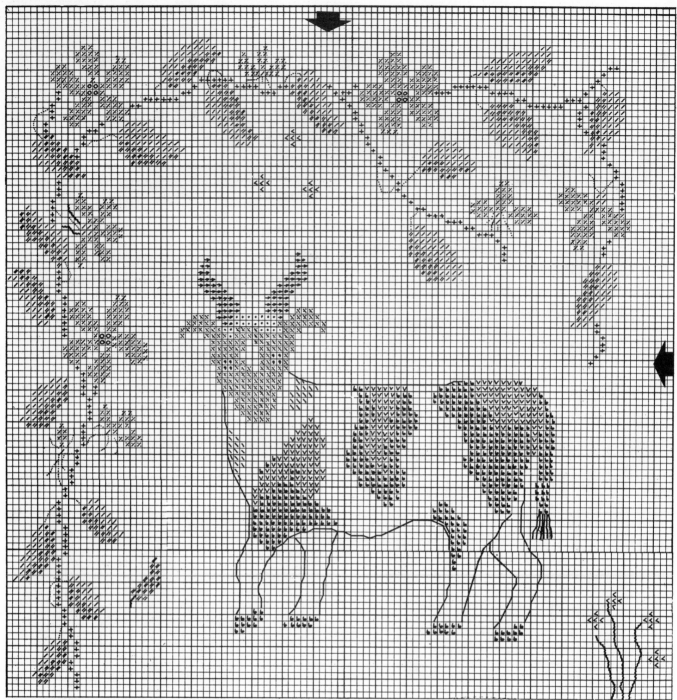

(See color illustration on inside front cover.)

taurus

april 20–may 21

DMC #

☑ 906 Medium Parrot Green	⊞ 611 Dark Drab Brown	◁ 676 Light Old Gold
⋯⋯ 906 Medium Parrot Green (backstitch)	· 415 Pearl Gray	⊠ { 414 Dark Steel Gray, 1 strand
☑ 905 Dark Parrot Green	◩ 318 Light Steel Gray	318 Light Steel Gray, 2 strands
⁓⁓ 905 Dark Parrot Green (backstitch)	⋁ 414 Dark Steel Gray	⬎ 807 Peacock Blue
☑ 350 Medium Coral	↳ 317 Pewter Gray	⊡ 347 Dark Salmon
	—— 317 Pewter Gray (backstitch)	
	⇥ 612 Medium Drab Brown	

When a symbol represents two colors, use the two together in the needle.

(See color illustration on inside front cover.)

Gemini
may 21–june 21

DMC #

H	334	Medium Bay Blue	- - -	989	Forest Green (backstitch)	{	3325	Baby Blue, 1 strand	
△	3325	Baby Blue	⊠	988	Medium Forest Green	⊠ {	334	Medium Bay Blue, 2 strands	
·	754	Light Peach Flesh	c	368	Light Pistachio Green				
◿	676	Light Old Gold	○	3326	Light Rose	—	309	Deep Rose (backstitch)	
⊡	725	Topaz	⧄	899	Medium Rose	⬚		Thread to match dress (backstitch)	
◿	611	Dark Drab Brown	⊓ {	776	Medium Pink, 1 strand				
∿	611	Dark Drab Brown (backstitch)	{	899	Medium Rose, 2 strands	·····	783	Christmas Gold (backstitch)	
			◿ {	783	Christmas Gold, 1 strand				
⊠	989	Forest Green	{	725	Topaz, 2 strands				

When a symbol represents two colors, use ~~the two~~ together in the needle.

(See color illustration on inside front cover.)

CANCER

JUNE 22–JULY 22

DMC #

▨	989	Forest Green
⊠	988	Medium Forest Green
◩	987	Dark Forest Green
⊡	503	Medium Blue Green
◪	3013	Light Khaki Green
⊙	892	Medium Carnation
◪	640	Very Dark Beige Gray

∿∿∿	892	Medium Carnation (backstitch)
⊡		White
⊠	840	Medium Beige Brown
——	840	Medium Beige Brown (backstitch)

◪	3041	Medium Antique Violet
----	3041	Medium Antique Violet (backstitch)
◁	676	Light Old Gold
◉	807	Peacock Blue
⊟	612	Medium Drab Brown

(See color illustration on inside front cover.)

Leo

July 23–August 22

DMC #		
� 355	Dark Terra Cotta	
⊻ 356	Medium Terra Cotta	
⊘ 3045	Dark Yellow Beige	
◢ 976	Medium Golden Brown	
— 976	Medium Golden Brown (backstitch)	
⊟ 989	Forest Green	
⧄ 988	Medium Forest Green	
◩ 437	Light Tan	

⧄ 977	Light Golden Brown	
⊡ 742	Light Tangerine	
⊡ 368	Light Pistachio Green	
⊠ 3347	Medium Yellow Green	
🄲 3346	Hunter Green	
◿ 676	Light Old Gold	
▽ { 355	Dark Terra Cotta, 1 strand	
356	Medium Terra Cotta, 2 strands	

⑴ { 976	Medium Golden Brown, 1 strand	
742	Light Tangerine, 2 strands	
◣ { 738	Very Light Tan, 1 strand	
435	Very Light Brown, 2 strands	
◩ { 738	Very Light Tan, 1 strand	
436	Tan, 2 strands	
◪ 518	Light Wedgwood	

When a symbol represents two colors, use the two together in the needle.

(See color illustration on inside front cover.)

VIRGO

august 23–september 23

DMC #

Symbol	#	Color		Symbol	#	Color
☒	3347	Medium Yellow Green		6	899	Medium Rose
----	3347	Medium Yellow Green (backstitch)		∿∿	899	Medium Rose (backstitch)
⧄	3346	Hunter Green		▨	813	Light Blue
⊙	334	Medium Bay Blue		—	813	Light Blue (backstitch on dress)
◿	676	Light Old Gold				
·	754	Light Peach Flesh		⊙ {	732	Olive Green, 1 strand
·	3326	Light Rose			3348	Light Yellow Green, 2 strands

Symbol	#	Color
⧄ {	3347	Medium Yellow Green, 1 strand
	3348	Light Yellow Green, 2 strands
V {	725	Topaz, 1 strand
	783	Christmas Gold, 2 strands
·······	783	Christmas Gold (backstitch)
+++	3326	Light Rose (backstitch)
9	986	Very Dark Forest Green

When a symbol represents two colors, use the two together in the needle.

(See color illustration on inside front cover.)

LIBRA

SEPTEMBER 24–OCTOBER 23

DMC #

·	368	Light Pistachio Green
∕	989	Forest Green
∕	988	Medium Forest Green
∕	986	Very Dark Forest Green
⁹	356	Medium Terra Cotta
—	356	Medium Terra Cotta (backstitch)
∅	732	Olive Green
∕	891	Dark Carnation

⋯⋯	891	Dark Carnation (backstitch)
◹	666	Bright Christmas Red
Ɪ	209	Dark Lavender
◉	208	Very Dark Lavender
◖	315	Dark Antique Mauve
—	315	Dark Antique Mauve (backstitch)

- - -	598	Light Turquoise (backstitch)
Ⅲ	597	Turquoise
∿∿	597	Turquoise (backstitch)
◁	676	Light Old Gold
V	726	Light Topaz
●	782	Medium Topaz
⊡	598	Light Turquoise

(See color illustration on inside front cover.)

SCORPIO

OCTOBER 24–NOVEMBER 21

DMC #

◹	906	Medium Parrot Green	⊞	783	Christmas Gold	◎	451	Dark Shell Gray
–––·	906	Medium Parrot Green (backstitch)	◖	781	Dark Topaz	—	451	Dark Shell Gray (backstitch)
☒	905	Dark Parrot Green	◿	453	Light Shell Gray	⊡	334	Medium Bay Blue
·······	905	Dark Parrot Green (backstitch)	●	602	Medium Cranberry	◸	676	Light Old Gold
			◢	840	Medium Beige Brown	⊡	725	Topaz
			◺	3041	Medium Antique Violet			

(See color illustration on inside front cover.)

SAGITTARIUS
NOVEMBER 22–DECEMBER 21

DMC #

⊡	989	Forest Green	⊞	518	Light Wedgwood	- - -	611	Dark Drab Brown (backstitch)
⊿	988	Medium Forest Green	◺	436	Tan	⊟	841	Light Beige Brown
⊠	986	Very Dark Forest Green	——	436	Tan (backstitch)	⩒	3045	Dark Yellow Beige
Ⅱ	504	Light Blue Green	⊘	435	Very Light Brown	◿	676	Light Old Gold
Ⅲ	503	Medium Blue Green	L	612	Medium Drab Brown	6	347	Dark Salmon
⊡	758	Light Terra Cotta	C	611	Dark Drab Brown	◪	356	Medium Terra Cotta
⊙	3328	Medium Salmon	◪	420	Dark Hazelnut Brown			

(See color illustration on inside front cover.)

CAPRICORN
December 22–January 20

DMC #

☑	3348	Light Yellow Green	
◪	3347	Medium Yellow Green	
◖	3346	Hunter Green	
◙	471	Very Light Avocado Green	
⋯⋯	471	Very Light Avocado Green (backstitch)	
◕	581	Moss Green	
◩	676	Light Old Gold	
◨	334	Medium Bay Blue	
⊞	453	Light Shell Gray	
▼	839	Dark Beige Brown	

	839	Dark Beige Brown (backstitch for mouth)
◧	840	Medium Beige Brown
⊠	841	Light Beige Brown
	841	Light Beige Brown (backstitch for whiskers)
⊟	842	Very Light Beige Brown
▨	451	Dark Shell Gray
▧	3023	Light Brown Gray
·⦃	368	Light Pistachio Green, 1 strand
		White, 2 strands

�	680	Dark Old Gold
⊠⦃	451	Dark Shell Gray, 1 strand
	453	Light Shell Gray, 2 strands
⊠⦃	3041	Medium Antique Violet, 1 strand
	3042	Light Antique Violet, 2 strands
⫫⦃	676	Light Old Gold, 1 strand
	680	Dark Old Gold, 2 strands

When a symbol represents two colors, use the two together in the needle.

(See color illustration on inside front cover.)

AQUARIUS
JANUARY 21–FEBRUARY 18

DMC #

◪	368	Light Pistachio Green
⊠	320	Medium Pistachio Green
◣	367	Dark Pistachio Green
⊞	3347	Medium Yellow Green
⊘	676	Light Old Gold
⊡	3325	Baby Blue
◪	334	Medium Bay Blue
◮	840	Medium Beige Brown

☑	841	Light Beige Brown
⊡	758	Light Terra Cotta
◪	3688	Medium Mauve
·····	3688	Medium Mauve (backstitch)
◢	3687	Mauve
——	3687	Mauve (backstitch)

9	420	Dark Hazelnut Brown
◪	369	Very Light Pistachio Green
◙ {	368	Light Pistachio Green, 1 strand
	307	Lemon, 2 strands
⊠	928	Light Gray Blue
◪	3022	Medium Brown Gray

When a symbol represents two colors, use the two together in the needle.

(See color illustration on inside front cover.)

pisces

february 19–march 20

DMC #

☒ 906	Medium Parrot Green	
◪ 3347	Medium Yellow Green	
⊡ 504	Light Blue Green	
◿ 503	Medium Blue Green	
◉ 502	Blue Green	
— 502	Blue Green (backstitch)	
◖ 501	Dark Blue Green	

∿ 501	Dark Blue Green (backstitch)	
⊡ 554	Light Violet	
◪ 553	Medium Violet	
▼ 552	Dark Violet	
➡ 976	Medium Golden Brown	

◹ 420	Dark Hazelnut Brown	
⊠ 841	Light Beige Brown	
Ⅴ {	553	Medium Violet, 1 strand
	552	Dark Violet, 2 strands
⋯⋯ 598	Light Turquoise (backstitch)	
◥ 676	Light Old Gold	

When a symbol represents two colors, use the two together in the needle.

48   ARBOR ZODIAC